Grace Lee Boggs

CHERRY LAKE PRESS

Published in the United States of America by Cherry Lake Publishing Group
Ann Arbor, Michigan
www.cherrylakepublishing.com

Reading Adviser: Beth Walker Gambro, MS, Ed., Reading Consultant, Yorkville, IL
Book Designer: Jennifer Wahi
Illustrator: Jeff Bane

Photo Credits: © Library of Congress/ LOC No. 2008678086/Detroit Photographic Co., 5; © Library of Congress/ LOC No. 94512334/Photo by Fred Palumbo, 7; © Richard Panasevich/Shutterstock, 9; © fizkes/Shutterstock, 11; © Thomas Margraf/Shutterstock, 13; © a katz/Shutterstock, 15; © Rena Schild/Shutterstock, 17; © Rawpixel.com/Shutterstock, 19; © Gary Stevens/flickr, 21; Jeff Bane, Cover, 1, 6, 8, 18; Various frames throughout, Shutterstock images

Cherry Lake Press is an imprint of Cherry Lake Publishing Group.

Library of Congress Cataloging-in-Publication Data

Names: Loh-Hagan, Virginia, author. | Bane, Jeff, 1957- illustrator.
Title: Grace Lee Boggs / by Virginia Loh-Hagan ; illustrated by Jeff Bane.
Description: Ann Arbor, Michigan : Cherry Lake Publishing Group, [2022] |
   Series: My itty-bitty bio | Includes bibliographical references and
   index. | Audience: Grades K-1
Identifiers: LCCN 2021036539 (print) | LCCN 2021036540 (ebook) | ISBN
   9781534198951 (hardcover) | ISBN 9781668900093 (paperback) | ISBN
   9781668905852 (ebook) | ISBN 9781668901533 (pdf)
Subjects: LCSH: Boggs, Grace Lee--Juvenile literature. | Chinese American
   women--Michigan--Detroit--Biography--Juvenile literature. | Chinese
   Americans--Michigan--Detroit--Biography--Juvenile literature. |
   Political activists--Michigan--Detroit--Biography--Juvenile literature.
   | Detroit (Mich.)--Biography--Juvenile literature.
Classification: LCC F574.D49 C55 2022 (print) | LCC F574.D49 (ebook) |
   DDC 305.48/8951073077434--dc23
LC record available at https://lccn.loc.gov/2021036539
LC ebook record available at https://lccn.loc.gov/2021036540

Printed in the United States of America
Corporate Graphics

About the author: When not writing, Dr. Virginia Loh-Hagan serves as the director of the Asian Pacific Islander Desi American (APIDA) Resource Center at San Diego State University. She identifies as Chinese American and is committed to amplifying APIDA communities. She lives in San Diego with her very tall husband and very naughty dogs.

About the illustrator: Jeff Bane and his two business partners own a studio along the American River in Folsom, California, home of the 1849 Gold Rush. When Jeff's not sketching or illustrating for clients, he's either swimming or kayaking in the river to relax.

My parents **emigrated** from China in 1911. I was born in 1915. I grew up in Rhode Island with six **siblings**.

I have an American and a Chinese name. My Chinese name means "Jade Peace."

What does your name mean?

I loved reading and writing in school. I got a **doctorate** in **philosophy**.

I could not get a job. I was an Asian American woman. No one would hire me. This was unfair.

I moved to Detroit, Michigan.
I married James Boggs. He was
an **activist**. We worked together.

My husband was Black. Black people were mistreated. This was wrong. I wanted to help them.

I stood up for workers and women. I stood up for poor people. I stood up for people of color.

Who do you stand up for?

I marched. I spoke. I wrote many books. I formed groups. I fought for **civil rights**.

I lived to be 100 years old. I died in 2015. But my **legacy** lives on. I continue to inspire others to fight for what is right.

What would you like to ask me?

1940

1915

↑
Born
1915

1953

2015

↑
Died
2015

glossary

activist (AK-tih-vist) a person who fights to bring about political or social change

civil rights (SIH-vuhl RITES) the rights of citizens to political and social freedom and equality

doctorate (DAHK-tuh-ruht) the highest degree awarded by a university

emigrated (EH-muh-gray-tuhd) left one country for another

legacy (LEH-guh-see) something handed down from one generation to another

philosophy (fuh-LAH-suh-fee) the study of truth, wisdom, and knowledge

siblings (SIH-blings) brothers and sisters

index